Angel Heart

From Heartbreak to Hope

Jodie Stevenson's Story

Shelley Wilburn

Angel Heart
From Heartbreak to Hope
Jodie Stevenson's Story

Copyright © 2024 Shelley Wilburn

First Edition
Nonfiction, Inspirational

All rights reserved. No part of this publication may be reproduced, stored in a retrieval system, or transmitted in any form or by any means, electronic, mechanical, photocopying, recording, or otherwise without the prior written permission of the author. Reviewers may quote briefly for review purposes.

All Scripture quotations, unless otherwise indicated, are taken from the New King James version. Scriptures marked NKJV are taken from the NEW KING JAMES VERSION (NKJV): Scripture taken from the NEW KING JAMES VERSION ® Copyright © 1982 by Thomas Nelson Inc. Used by permission. All rights reserved.

Scriptures marked NLT are taken from the HOLY BIBL, NEW LIVING TRANSLATION (NLT): Scriptures taken from the HOLY BIBLE, NEW LIVING TRANSLATION, Copyright © 1996, 2004, 2007, by Tyndale House Foundation. Used by permission of Tyndale House Publishers, Inc., Carol Stream, Illinois 60188. All rights reserved. Used by permission.

Understanding Grief from Pain to Purpose by Tina Porter, M.A., QMHP, B.S.W., Grief, Trauma & Mental Health Expert

Chapter head images by Shelley Wilburn, courtesy of Canva.com
Cover design by Paul Ruane
ISBN: 978-0-9864311-8-0

Written, edited, and formatted by Shelley Wilburn, Walking Healed Ministries and Mountain Joy Publishing
Published by Mountain Joy Publishing

Printed in the United States of America

Angel Heart

Dedication

This story is dedicated to anyone who has lost a child. May God comfort you in knowing that He holds you and your Angel Heart close.

Contents

	Acknowledgments	viii
	Introduction	ix
1	**Waiting is the Hardest Part**	1
2	**Born Too Early**	9
3	**Tiny Fighter**	17
4	**Saying Goodbye**	22
5	**Final Farewell**	25
	Message From Jodie	27
	Afterword	29
	Bonus Material	31
	Angel Heart 5-Day Devotional	33
	Appendix A	46

- Understanding Grief

	Appendix B	52

- Libbi's Song

Appendix C	54
• The Speeches	
Endnotes	56
About the Author	59
Other Titles by Shelley Wilburn	61
Picture Gallery	64

Acknowledgements

We want to give special acknowledgement to the doctors and nurses who cared for Jodie during her pregnancy and delivery of our baby. To the Fetal Care in Carbondale, and especially the medical staff, doctors and nurses at Cardinal Glennon Hospital, you are all so special to us. Also, a very special thank you to Dr. Claassen for noticing our learning disabilities and taking the time to explain things in detail, as well as writing things down so we could understand. We will always be thankful for our "Angel Doctor."

~ Jodie and Willie Stevenson

Introduction

I met Jodie Stevenson one day when I was meeting with a mutual friend, and sister-in-Christ. She had been speaking with Jodie regarding the loss of her baby when Jodie mentioned wanting to write a book about her experience. She had a desire to be able to help and minister to other young women who had lost a baby. Knowing my background in writing, editing, and publishing, my friend thought it would be in our best interest that Jodie and I meet. Maybe I could help her to write her book. Little did I know what God had planned for both of us!

Before you begin reading, I want you, the reader, to know some things about this book, and about Jodie.

When Jodie told me she had written a book, she wanted me to see what I thought about it and give her some pointers on what to do next. She emailed it to me. When I saw it, I knew something was different about her. Her verbiage revealed something that, in doing some investigating, revealed a learning disability, to which Jodie, herself, later admitted. In the coming weeks, I would come to know the extent of that issue.

I suggested she come to me for coaching on writing, so I could help teach her the basics of writing in order to help her get her story written the way she wanted it to be told. As I met with Jodie, she tried hard to learn and understand so she could write her book.

However, as the weeks progressed, things weren't happening that way. One day Jodie told me, "When I was in school, I had to take Special Ed because I have a learning disability. I really try hard to do things, but my grammar and words don't come out right. It's hard for me."

In that instant, the Lord spoke to my heart and said, *"You write this book."*

The already sweet relationship I was building with Jodie began to shift. I always saw her as a very loving and sweet girl. That didn't change. However, on this day, I became very protective of her and the story she wanted the world to hear. We talked about that and how we both felt, then she agreed to allow me to write the book *for* her; to do it in a way that would get her story out there but to also, hopefully, minister to others. She wanted people to know the real Jodie, her learning disabilities, as well as the hurt, confusion, and heartbreak she has endured.

Many people don't see those who have learning disabilities as people who can function in "the real world." But God made Jodie and her husband, Willie, just as He made the rest of us. They are not a mistake, nor a failure. They have feelings and emotions like everyone else. They can work, serve, cook, clean, drive, make decisions, and do all the things others do. Even more, they can *love*. In my experience, they love deeper and with more intensity.

Jodie doesn't want sympathy. In one of our meetings she said, "I don't want people to feel sorry for me. I just want people to know that I'm a person, and I have feelings, too. I know what it feels like to lose a baby. It hurt me deeply. And I want people to know my story and know my Libbi. I want to give comfort to other hurting women out there who have lost a baby."

I interviewed Jodie that day and wrote several pages of notes. I asked deeply personal questions and allowed her to answer in her own way. Jodie referred to her baby, Libbi, as her *Angel Heart*. Hence, the title of this book. After our interview, I then wrote *Angel Heart* in a short, simple way, using personal quotes from Jodie in order to tell her story.

Angel Heart is not a lengthy book, but it's filled with the raw emotion of a young mother who endured watching her premature baby fight for life, and then allowed the God she believes in, loves, and serves to give that baby the ultimate healing, which was taking her back into Heaven where Jodie knows that someday, she will see Libbi again.

Our prayer is that as you read *Angel Heart*, you will be comforted and encouraged, but that you will also see Jodie and Willie with new eyes. We want you to know them as a young, married couple who genuinely loved their baby, and who were heartbroken over their loss, but because they love and serve Jesus, they trusted Him enough to let her go.

I have also included a 5-day devotional at the end of this book, to help encourage you in your own healing of the heart.

~ Shelley Wilburn
Founder of Walking Healed Ministries and Mountain Joy Publishing, Author, Speaker, Writer, Editor, and Pastoral Minister at Purpose House Church

Angel Heart

1 - Waiting is the Hardest Part

Trust in the LORD with all your heart, And lean not on your own understanding; In all your ways acknowledge Him, And He shall direct your paths.
~ Proverbs 3:5-6, NKJV

Waiting is hard.

Jodie Stevenson grew up in the little village of Crab Orchard in Southern Illinois. A sweet girl, she just wanted to love someone, to be loved, and to someday be a mommy.

Nearly every little girl dreams of finding her knight in shining armor – the whole princess being rescued from the castle tower by her knight on a white horse. As she grows up, those fairytale dreams sort of come true when she puts on the beautiful, sparkling prom dress and is escorted to prom by her handsome beau.

However, the wait between grade school to high school can be long. When that same little girl is diagnosed with a learning disability, her wait can seem to take a lifetime. It was this way for Jodie. As much as she dreamed of someday going to prom, she didn't know if that would happen, but she was determined that a learning disability would not stop her.

In 2016, with prom nearing and yet, no date, Jodie's cousin set her up to meet a boy named William (Willie) Stevenson. Jodie would later refer to him as her "red-haired man."

They met at the local Dairy Queen where her cousin introduced them. They hit it off and the prom date was set. Jodie was about to realize at least one of her dreams.

As she explained, it was just supposed to be for prom. But afterwards, they went their separate ways... and Jodie was devastated. She had fallen in love with Willie and didn't want to see him go.

In her words, "I was very hurt and broken. I just kept working through it, but it was so hard to do because Willie is forever my dream. To me, he was the only one I loved."

After high school, Jodie tried to move on with her life. She enrolled in college at Southern Illinois University in Carbondale (SIUC) but, as she put it, "it didn't work out for me."

From grade school through high school, Jodie explained that she had to be in the Special Education program due to her having difficulty learning and understanding. Therefore, college was even more of a challenge.

Jodie realized that college wasn't for her. She remembered the struggle she had throughout school, because of how hard it had been for her to understand and learn. Therefore, she knew dropping out of college was the right thing to do.

Rather than college, Jodie got a job in a nursing home, doing laundry. But she just couldn't stop thinking about her *red-haired man*.

She decided to work and to pray and trust God to bring Willie back into her life. Praying and praising God is what got her through. She loves to praise God. One day, when we were talking, Jodie told me that praising God is such a beautiful thing and puts a person at peace. She knew it would be God's timing and not hers if she and Willie were to reunite.

She also knew her skills and what she loved to do, which is why she got the job in the nursing home.

"I love doing laundry," she explains. "It gives me joy to know I'm helping others."

Growing up, Jodie would clean house for her parents. But growing up also wasn't easy for her. Having many difficulties understanding things, she felt she was not always accepted, not only by peers, but sometimes even from family. She often felt left out and unappreciated in the things she did for others.

Jodie wished for someone of her own to love, which now included Willie and, someday, a baby.

She would wait. She decided that, while waiting, she would keep working and try to move on with her life.

It would be three years before Jodie would hear from Willie again.

~

In 2019, Jodie received a surprise when Willie messaged her. He asked her out on a date, to which she gladly accepted. After getting to know one another again, they realized they were meant to be together.

In May of 2020, Willie proposed. Jodie was about to realize more of her dream of being married and beginning a life together with her red-haired man.

Sadly, not everyone was supportive of Jodie and Willie's marriage. However, the two overcame and set their wedding date for the Fall of 2020.

Jodie told me, "I love Fall. Everything about Fall reminds me of just God's beauty. [I love] Rose Gold. It is like the color pink. Beauty!"

Although it was Covid season, Jodie and Willie thought they would have to cancel their wedding. They were even told they couldn't get married. But the two were adamant about it, therefore, on October 24, 2020, Jodie and Willie were married.

"It was the best day ever!" Jodie related.

After a short honeymoon in Nashville, Tennessee, Willie and Jodie began their life together in the small town of Goreville, Illinois, where Willie grew up. But things were not as happy as Jodie would have liked.

Although she and Willie were happy, there were some who still didn't support them as well as she would have liked. She still wanted to be a mommy, but many people wanted her on birth control. That deeply hurt her.

"I have every right to be a mommy," Jodie would tell them. "Me and Willie will always be there for each other. I'm just excited to be with [him] and no one else. I will always love my husband and our kids. But the main part is God first and forever most."

She determined in her heart to prove them wrong. After their short honeymoon, they both went to work, Jodie at the nursing home, and Willie to FedEx, which they both loved.

Jodie always wanted to be a housewife, take care of the house and kids. She said, "I was made for this." It grieved her to have to go to work, because she wanted to be home cooking, cleaning, and taking care of children. However, she also wanted to help her husband pay bills, so she worked as they began trying to build their little family.

The Joy and the Hurt

In October of 2021, Jodie began not feeling well. She had a cough, but she kept thinking there was something more to it than just that. At her job, the employees were required to submit to a weekly Covid test. Jodie submitted to the test but thought no more of it. Later, she received a call telling her the Covid test came back positive.

She still had a feeling something else was going on, so she did a home pregnancy test. It was positive.

She was excited to discover she was pregnant. Her dream of being a mommy had begun. However, again, not everyone was as happy as Jodie and Willie that they were going to be parents.

One thing Jodie heard, which hurt her deeply was, "Get an abortion." This broke her heart. Why couldn't everyone be happy for her? All she dreamed in life was to be a mommy.

In talking to her, Jodie smiled and said, "Never let anyone live rent-free in your head." Her motto became, *Healthy Mom, Healthy Baby*. She fully believed that in her heart. She was determined to become a mommy, and a good mommy, to this baby she now carried.

Jodie and Willie were happy. She was so excited that she already had names picked out for the baby, both boy and girl names. She decided she would ignore comments from other people, even though it hurt her feelings. Regardless of what anyone said to them, Jodie and Willie determined they were going to be good parents to this precious baby.

Complications

Everything with the pregnancy was fine through their doctor's appointment in November. However, beginning in January and into February, they received news which began to confuse and hurt both Jodie and Willie.

During an ultrasound, at one doctor's appointment, they were told, "We can't find the baby's heartbeat."

Confused and afraid, they didn't know what that meant. Did the technician not know what she was doing? Was the equipment not working? Why couldn't they find the baby's heartbeat? No one explained to them so they could understand.

Instead, Jodie and Willie were transferred to the Fetal Care in Carbondale. At the Fetal Care, Jodie and Willie had a FaceTime call with a doctor and were told their baby had a hole in her heart. Jodie did not understand what that meant but knew in her mommy heart that something wasn't adding up. Everything had been fine up to this point in her pregnancy.

They had even had the gender reveal and discovered the baby was a girl. Jodie was so excited! She could envision pretty, little dresses, pink everything, teaching her little girl about things, watching her grow up. She imagined her little girl becoming a cheerleader, going to ballgames to watch her cheer. She even imagined the beautiful dresses she would wear to proms, all the sparkle and glitter and so much more. Jodie couldn't wait to see her dream come true. Only now, she was being told her baby has a hole in her heart and they were being transferred yet again. They would have to go to Cardinal Glennon Children's Hospital in St. Louis, where they would wait for more testing and more answers.

At Cardinal Glennon, Jodie and Willie were told there was no hole in their baby's heart. However, before they could be relieved, they were told that instead, the baby only had three heart chambers rather than four. Their baby would need surgery when she was born.

Jodie and Willie were overwhelmed with a lot of information and a lot of people; doctors, nurses, family members, giving and wanting information. Everyone wanted to know what was going on and Jodie just wasn't able to give it. She herself was overwhelmed, confused, hurt, and didn't know what to do. However, she and Willie kept going to the doctor's appointments and waiting and praying to see how the baby would develop. Always, in her heart of hearts, Jodie hoped this would resolve and her baby would be fine.

~

In April, she started having issues with her pregnancy. She started swelling and her blood pressure became high. At one doctor's appointment they discovered the baby's heart rate had elevated and was beating too fast. The baby was in distress.

Jodie was rushed to Carbondale hospital where they determined she had Pre-Eclampsia. Generally, this can be treated or managed with oral or IV medications until the baby has developed enough to be delivered. However, because her heart was beating too fast, and she was in distress, Jodie would need to deliver her quickly and safely for both she and the baby.

The medical staff began procedures to help Jodie deliver, nevertheless, when they administered the epidural, it didn't work. She would have to have an emergency C-Section to deliver the baby in order to save her.

Jodie was immediately taken into surgery for her C-Section and put under anesthesia.

1 - Born Too Early

*Guard your heart above all else, for it determines
the course of your life.
~ Proverbs 4:23, NLT*

Libbi Grace Stevenson was born on April 13, 2022, at thirty-three weeks. She weighed three pounds, fourteen ounces and was sixteen-and-a-half inches long.

Jodie felt as if she slept for many hours after her C-Section. When she awoke, she began screaming, "Where's my baby!" All she wanted was to hold her precious baby.

She was disappointed, as well as confused, when they wheeled Libbi into her room, because the baby was in an incubator, connected to a breathing tube, and wires to monitor her and keep her alive. Jodie was unable to hold her precious baby. Jodie and Willie could only look at their Libbi through the little incubator.

Jodie said, "I wanted to scream, 'Why, why, why?! Why does my baby have to be this way? Why do other sweet parents' babies have to be this way?' The pain is real. Seeing my baby having so many wires and tubes and such, it hurt me so much."

Then, as quick as they wheeled Libbi in, they took her away again and transferred her to Cardinal Glennon so she could begin receiving the extended care she desperately needed.

Jodie was devastated, wanting to be with her baby.

"I'm her mommy! She needs to be with me!" she cried.

Later, she would tell me, "I was hurt more and more. Pain is so real, and hurt, and grief. But I know that I know, God holds the days and numbers of family and friends. God is the God of miracles, so be still and know He is God."

Regardless, after the C-Section, Jodie had some healing of her own to do before she could be released from the hospital. She had to accomplish a few things to make sure her body was healing. She was to report her progress to the nurses and/or doctor in order to be discharged.

The next morning, Jodie, determined to be released from the hospital, lied to the nurses and said she had accomplished what they said she needed to do. Soon afterward, she was released from the hospital, with congratulations on her baby, and sent her on her way.

Jodie and Willie went home to pack their bags so they could get to Cardinal Glennon to see Libbi and find out what was going on. Jodie needed to see her baby. She also could barely walk after having her C-Section. However, she was one determined mommy.

~

Once at the hospital, they were told they had to scrub to get into the NICU to see Libbi. This caused more confusion for both Jodie and Willie. Jodie didn't understand why they had to scrub, nor why they had to wear face masks.

"It's my baby and we have the same germs," she argued. She didn't understand that even a slight runny nose, or cough, could be detrimental to Libbi, or to the other babies in the NICU.

While at the hospital, they needed support and encouragement more than ever. Jodie and Willie discovered there were Chaplains who would come in and pray for them and with them, supporting them in their hurt and grief. To Jodie, they were amazing. She needed those prayers, not only for Libbi, but for herself. She and Willie were very thankful for the prayers.

They were also very thankful that they finally got to hold Libbi. Jodie kept saying that Libbi needed their love and to know her parents.

She began to feel the support for herself and her little family through the support of the doctors, nurses, and chaplains.

Yet, she also didn't understand when the doctors kept saying, "Your baby is at risk." What did that mean? Jodie and Willie didn't understand that with three heart chambers, Libbi's heart wasn't beating properly, nor was she breathing on her own. Libbi was at risk for not surviving.

Libbi also had other physical and health issues that they did not understand. Jodie was confused and hurt, as well as heartbroken. She didn't know why no one was explaining things to her in terms she could understand. In her hurt and brokenness, she began to think the doctors and nurses just didn't want her to know, and that they were keeping her from getting to hold her baby more.

Jodie kept telling them that her baby needed to be held. She needed to know that she was loved.

Jodie's phone would also keep going off with messages from family wanting to know information that she couldn't give. She was so overwhelmed by all the questions being asked, as well as the information the doctors were giving her.

At one point in the NICU, as Jodie said, "an angel doctor came in who was a joy and had compassion" for she and Willie. Jodie explained, "Willie and [I] are the same. We have learning disabilities, and we don't understand a lot of things. But this angel doctor, came in and she figured it out. She began writing things down for us. She explained things better for us and helped us to try to understand. She was amazing and pure joy, which made it easy for me and Willie and our little Libbi. I wanted to ask, 'Where were you all this time?'"

Dr. Claassen, the angel doctor, noticed Willie and Jodie were struggling to understand what was being said to them about their baby, Libbi. That's when she took them aside and began explaining the situation, giving them details, and trying to make it easier for them. She would write things down and have them look things up to try to help educate Jodie and Willie on the things Libbi was going through.

It might have taken a while, but as Jodie said, "By Jesus' blood, and His grace, we can do it! It sure hurt to watch my sweet baby girl with all the wires and tubes. I never wanted for me or her dad to stop holding her. I just wanted to keep on holding her [and never let her go]. But [Willie and I] had to get freshened up and take care of ourselves as well, which was so hard to do.

Willie went to work for us to support Libbi and me. I thank God for that!

"Everyone gave us gifts and such to support us as well, which is very kind. I was overwhelmed by it all. Willie would come on the weekends to stay with Libbi and me, to see his precious baby girl."

At one point, Willie told Jodie she needed to get a break from the hospital and go back home. He knew she was missing home, which she was, but she didn't want to leave her baby. The hospital staff told Jodie it was okay for her to leave, and that Libbi would be in good hands. They assured her that it was okay for her to take a break. Before she left, they gave Jodie the phone number and told her they would call if there was an emergency. So, Jodie and Willie left to go back home for a little while.

Although she came home, that first night she woke up crying because she missed her sweet baby. So, she called the hospital to check up on Libbi before they went back. She was given a good report that all was going smooth, and the reports were great for the baby.

"Keep it up, baby girl!" Jodie cheered for Libbi.

The next day, they headed back to St. Louis. When they arrived to see Libbi, Jodie turned around and went to the bathroom, crying.

When Willie caught up with her, he asked what was wrong. Jodie explained that she didn't like "that black, evil [thing]" which was in their way of seeing Libbi. The black thing was an oxygen bottle which was giving Libbi the air she needed in order to breathe. It hurt her heart to see so many things attached to her tiny, sweet baby.

"I was just thinking about Mary, Jesus' mother, how Jesus was getting torn up on the cross, and Mary was crying, seeing Him that way. That was me; so hurt and broken. The pain hurts! I just always questioned, 'Why us, honey? Why? We are married. We know how to nurse.' But we can't give up hope when we wanted to give up. We have to keep trusting and obeying God! I even told my husband we have an enemy somewhere and I will stand my ground where hope will be found! We will not give up on our sweet daughter. She is a warrior. She is strong forever and ever.

"The encouragement that really cheered me on was seeing Libbi's doctor write some good words on Libbi's board in the NICU. God almost took Libbi home while she was in the NICU, but we just kept praising His name.

"We let the doctors do what they had to do. I know Libbi was definitely a miracle to them as well and her dad and me. The entire family, actually," Jodie said.

Guard Your Heart

Libbi needed heart surgery. There was no way around it. However, her surgery kept getting put off due to her tiny size. She needed to be a certain weight before the doctors could safely operate on her. Libbi weighed three pounds, fourteen ounces at birth. She needed to at least weigh seven pounds or more before surgery could happen. But could she gain that much weight?

Jodie was able to pump breast milk to feed Libbi and help try to get her weight up so she could have her surgery.

When the day came for Libbi's first surgery on May 18, 2022, Jodie cried. She wanted her baby to be safe. She tried to understand why her baby had to have surgery, but she was tired. It scared her because Libbi was still tiny, and she didn't want to lose her baby.

"I will never handle it well," she said.

"We prayed and prayed when she went for surgery. Trust, trust, trust in God and have faith. It was scary enough for me, but I held onto my cross. The Bible says to take up the cross and follow Jesus. The world desperately needs Jesus!

"We just waited on the reports from the surgeons. Waiting is hard, but waiting is also beautiful. When the surgeons came to the waiting room, they told us about our sweet daughter and had no negative reports! We thanked God for that win.

"But it wasn't over yet. We still had a long way to go.

"Positive. Positive is what we needed to hear, but we still have to be still and know He is God and He is the Doctor [Great Physician].

"The amazing thing is that Libbi was in room seven. Seven is Jesus' number in the PICU. Libbi kept pushing it to the limit. We are made to win! Win with Jesus!

"We got to see our sweet, beautiful baby girl when surgery was over. Oh, my sweet baby was so swollen, and the wires and tubes were still there. It hurt this momma's heart.

"In order to see her or to get close, we had to wear our face masks, and I didn't like that one bit."

~

Jodie still didn't understand the need for the face masks. In her mind, she, Willie, and Libbi all had the same germs. Therefore, she was mad about the masks, still not realizing that any symptoms could be life-threatening to Libbi.

Willie and Jodie were tired after waiting so long while Libbi was in surgery. After seeing her, they left the hospital and went to Ronald McDonald House to rest and sleep before going back to the hospital.

They got up early (6:00AM) to head back to the hospital, only to discover that Libbi's heart had stopped in the night, and she had to be put on ECMO.

At this point, Jodie told Willie she was going to get her things from Ronald McDonald House and bring to the hospital because she decided she would not leave Libbi alone again.

The next morning Jodie awoke to see Libbi's eyes wide open, and she was awake. How precious to get to see her baby's beautiful eyes. To Jodie, this was a win. Such a beautiful testimony.

Through watching all that her daughter was going through Jodie realized she needed to guard her own heart as well.

3 - Tiny Fighter

*My flesh and my heart fail; But God is the strength of
my heart and my portion forever.
~ Psalms 73:26, NKJV*

Through all the surgeries and dialysis that Libbi underwent, Jodie kept hearing, "Your baby is at risk." She knew her baby was struggling, but in her own heart and mind she kept believing that Libbi was fighting for life. Therefore, she didn't understand why the doctors and nurses kept telling them that Libbi was at risk. At risk for what?

They were told that Libbi would only have heart surgery. However, Libbi had to have multiple surgeries.

Jodie felt as if the doctors and nurses lied to them – although, in truth, they didn't understand that, as the doctors worked on Libbi, they would discover more issues which were wrong in her little body. Those included not only her heart, but her lungs, and her kidneys, for which she would have to have dialysis.

Libbi was put on ECMO to help her breathe.

Jodie was so hurt over what her baby was enduring. She was also confused over it all. She has stated repeatedly that she and Willie have learning disabilities, therefore they have a hard time understanding many things. But they try.

Libbi did get off the ECMO for a short time. But she had to go back on it because she couldn't breathe on her own. Her little lungs just weren't developed enough for her to be able to breathe by herself.

Libbi fought through everything, surgeries, dialysis, ECMO, etc. It was heartbreaking for them to see their baby that way.

Although they didn't understand, Jodie and Willie complied with the hospital rules of washing their hands and wearing face masks. They wanted to be near their baby.

Even so, with all the precautions, Libbi got an infection while in the NICU. Again, Jodie didn't understand how this could have happened.

It was explained to her that, even with all the precautions taken to keep a sterile environment for the baby, infections can still happen.

Jodie explained, "Our sweet girl went through so much on her tiny body. We needed to get the fluids off her. She went through so many surgeries, not just heart surgery, but peritoneal dialysis surgery. She fought that hard, like a champ. Libbi was such a miracle."

~

June 14, 2022

On this day, the family was called to the hospital. Jodie and Willie wanted to have Libbi baptized. The hospital graciously provided a pretty, little, "white shiny dress" in which Libbi could be baptized, with her family gathered around.

Still connected to ECMO, wires, tubes and such, Willie and Jodie felt at ease over having their daughter baptized.

"She looked so beautiful in her white, shiny dress. It's what I had always dreamed of seeing her in," Jodie said, with a proud smile.

All seemed well in the world after having Libbi baptized. Jodie and Willie felt better than they had since Libbi was born and through all their baby had endured thus far.

But their happiness was short-lived.

In Jodie's words, "We all know God answers prayers. We all know Libbi is strong and mighty, but the reports kept on getting us negative results. Basically, they kept saying to us that we either watch Libbi get off the ECMO machine and she will just pass away, or [we can] hold our sweet baby – to remove the wires and tubes and she will pass away. They kept telling me that my Libbi was going to pass away.

"I kept believing that it was not up to the doctors to say when Libbi would pass. It was God's. I wanted the Lord to prove them wrong!"

~

On June 15, 2022, when Jodie awoke, she noticed that Libbi's heart rate was very low. When she asked the nurse about it, she was told, "Your baby had a seizure on the ECMO machine."

The doctor came in and explained to Jodie and Willie that their baby was not going to survive. They were told that Libbi was going to pass. It was just a matter of time.

Jodie left the room, crying.

She went to the Chapel where she began praying out

Angel Heart

loud, talking to God. She begged God, and began asking, "What do I do? I'm so confused." She asked God for answers while she walked around the darkened Chapel, praying and crying.

~

When Jodie went back to Libbi's room, she and Willie talked about what they needed to do, and they made a decision. They would take Libbi off the ECMO.

They had been watching for two months and enduring their daughter's heartbreaking fight for life. They were tired, confused, hurt, and heartbroken. They also knew Libbi was tired. They no longer wanted to see her suffer. They just wanted to hold Libbi.

Jodie went to the doctor and said, "I can't deal with this anymore. I'm tired of the hurt, the pain, and the confusion. I want to hold my baby. She needs to know she's loved."

Jodie says it was the toughest decision she and Willie had to make. So, they called all the family again to let them know what was going on and so they could have the support of family surrounding them and Libbi, although not all of them could be in the room. Jodie thought the hospital kept changing the policies on how many people could be in the room, but the hospital staff just didn't want the room to be overcrowded.

Jodie kept saying, "It's *my* baby." She was also having to endure questions and suggestions coming from family members, which caused her great stress and anxiety. What they were about to do would be life changing as well as heartbreaking.

Jodie remembers saying, "It's not my decision. It's not my idea that my baby is like this. This is not my fault."

On the day of their decision, the doctors and nurses

came in to take Libbi off the ECMO. They tried to prepare them for what would happen when they took the breathing tube out. They explained that Libbi would pass quietly, because she was just so tiny, she had multiple physical issues, and she just wasn't strong enough to survive. They wanted to make sure they both understood and tried to prepare them. It was heartbreaking for everyone involved, and the doctors and nurses cried with Willie and Jodie.

Everyone left the room to allow the doctors and nurses to do their work and process things. The family went into the waiting room. They cried and prayed as they waited. It was such a heartbreaking time.

When the medical staff was done, Jodie and Willie were allowed back into the room.

Jodie remembers looking up at Libbi's heart rate, to find it was beating normally.

"I'm not giving up hope on my beautiful daughter," she said.

The nurse explained everything to her, but Jodie kept praying, asking God to prove the doctors wrong.

"It's up to You and Libbi, Lord."

However, when the nurse took out Libbi's breathing tube, a surprising thing happened. Libbi didn't pass right away. In fact, she began blowing bubbles. Jodie believed Libbi was fighting to live.

She remembers smiling at Willie and saying, "Look at that. She's strong like me and you. She's a tiny fighter."

They handed Libbi to Willie, and Jodie leaned in to get a good, up close look at their sweet baby. All they could do was stare at this precious gift.

Their lives were about to change forever.

4 - Saying Goodbye

The LORD is close to the brokenhearted; he rescues those whose spirits are crushed.
~ Psalms 34:18, NLT

After a few moments holding Libbi, Willie suddenly told Jodie, "Honey, we have to stand up."

"Willie, I can't stand up." Jodie was still recovering from her C-Section, so standing was difficult for her.

Willie was adamant. "Stand up!"

Realizing what was happening, Jodie couldn't bear to see. She turned her back and began crying.

~

Jodie explained that Willie stood up and turned toward the window of Libbi's hospital room. When he did, he looked out and saw Jesus, and his grandma and grandpa Stevenson, standing at the gates of Heaven, welcoming their great-granddaughter. Their arms were outstretched toward Willie and Libbi.

When they reached for Libbi, Willie lifted her up toward his grandparents. As he did, he passed out on the floor still holding Libbi (he did not drop her).

Not long after, Jodie ran from the room, screaming, and ran into a darkened conference room. She quickly pulled up the song, *Scars in Heaven* and played it while she grieved the loss of her baby. That song gave her some peace in her heart.

A nurse had followed her into the room and tried to console her, then led her back to the room, where Jodie asked the nurse if she could get everyone out of the room except for Willie, Jodie, and Jodie's cousin. She wanted alone time to say goodbye to Libbi.

Jodie knew that Libbi was gone, but she still held her baby and loved on her one last time.

~

Later, Jodie related when Willie fainted onto the floor with Libbi still in his hands, his dad picked her up. Jodie had asked for the baby, and Willie's dad handed Libbi to her.

"They let me hold her. Then the nurse took her, and I had to go run."

Jodie explained that, during Willie's vision, Libbi passed away. She firmly believes that Willie handed Libbi into the hands of his grandparents.

"They reached for Libbi and Willie handed her to them. Then he fainted. She had passed," she explained, with tears in her eyes.

She also explained that her mom later told her that when Willie stood up with Libbi and turned around, she looked, and his face was glowing. Then, she saw a bright light coming through the window.

Jodie didn't see all of that because she had turned away as her heart was breaking. She was focused on her baby's passing.

She explained, "[When everyone was out of the

room, we held our Libbi]. We gave her kisses, then packed our things, said goodbye, and went back to the Ronald McDonald house and slept. It was painful to sleep. There was so much heartache, crying, and screaming. But through it all, it was God and Libbi.

"I know Jesus. And I knew this was going to happen. I didn't want to, because I wanted to see our plans for her. She was strong just like me and Willie. But she fought. She was a tiny fighter. Libbi went to be with Jesus on June 15, 2022."

5 - Final Farewell

*He heals the brokenhearted
And binds up their wounds.
~ Psalms 147:3, NKJV*

After saying their goodbyes to Libbi, Jodie and Willie came back home to plan Libbi's funeral. It wasn't something they looked forward to doing, yet it had to be done.

There were many who wanted to help the two plan their baby's funeral, but Jodie was adamant that she wanted to do it.

"For Libbi's special day, we will wear pink," she said.

She wanted Libbi's funeral to be at the church where she attended family gatherings. Libbi's burial would be in the town where her husband, Willie, had grown up: Goreville, Illinois.

Jodie said the reason she chose Goreville was because she loves the town, but also that is where Libbi's daddy was raised and grew up.

"It's just sad that I would not be able to see my baby girl being a Goreville Blackcat cheerleader. But I know she is a cheerleader up in Heaven with Jesus!

"I thank God that He let us have our sweet baby girl for at least two months here on Earth, to love on her and to look at the impact she made through me and Willie."

Jodie *went all out* for Libbi's funeral. She chose a *fancy* stone with lambs. She wanted to preserve her daughter's memory in the best way she could.

"I know Libbi was very special to all. Still, the pain hurts," she said.

Message from Jodie

No matter what you go through – because this life, it's crazy sometimes – just hold on with Jesus. That's all I can say. I didn't plan for this to happen. After Libbi passed, we wrote a song for her. We call it Libbi's Song. They played it. Music therapy helped us. I also wrote a speech to say at Libbi's funeral.

Grief never goes away, because you love. I don't wish for anybody to go through what we went through. Because it's just heartache. [Libbi] was just two months old. It's hard. But I thank God every step of the way that He let us hold her and let us get to be with her. But I know if I keep my faith and keep going, [like] what the Bible says: keep the faith and keep going, keep running the race – I'll get to see my baby again in Heaven.

I'm just here for me and my husband and what we need. We're doing okay. It's hard. Most married couples couldn't do what we did or what we went through. Sometimes I just want it to go away. I wish the thirteenth of every month would go away. My husband knows when I'm going to grieve and wishes I wouldn't. Grieving is hard. You never get over it. People tell me, "It's over and done with and you just need to get over it." But she was my baby. They didn't have her, I did. They don't understand the pain I go through. I tell them, "Your pain is different from my pain." Those who tell you they 'got over it,' they really didn't. They're processing their grief through anger. Then, I get mad.

Sometimes people say hurtful things and they may not mean to ... but they also might mean it. Sometimes you just have to walk away. You can still love those people – but you don't have to be best friends with them. Don't let them have control in your life or control you.

I don't want people to feel sorry for me. I want people to know that, even though Willie and I have learning disabilities, we can still love. We can still be good parents. We may not understand a lot of things, but we do understand loving each other and loving a baby and taking care of that baby the best that we can.

I know this: Jesus can make a broken heart, beat again.

Afterword

It was an absolute joy getting to work with Jodie on this project. Although heartbreaking, I know her story will help many who will have the privilege of reading about her journey.

I learned much about Jodie as we met each week. She has a beautiful personality and a heart to help others. It gives her great joy to know she was able to do something for someone which either helped to take care of that person or gave them joy, even if it's doing their laundry and keeping them in clean bedsheets. It also makes her feel good to know she is appreciated for the work she does.

Since the loss of her baby, it has become Jodie's great desire to minister comfort to other women who are grieving the loss of a child. Many times, throughout our meetings, she would talk about wanting to help others.

Another thing Jodie and I would talk about is how she felt about the way people react to her due to her learning disability. In working with her, I discovered a young woman whose heart hurts over things people say to her, and the way she is treated because she often doesn't understand things.

It's my experience that Jodie just learns differently than others, only at a much slower pace. However, she is not dumb. On the contrary. She is a very conscientious young woman. She's alert, but cautious. Because of things in her past, and experience with other people, she doesn't readily trust, or open up. Yet, when she realizes she can trust you, she opens that beautiful personality and blossoms. Her smile is beautiful. Her laugh is contagious. If she likes you, she loves you, and does so with enthusiasm.

At our first meeting, as we were getting to know one another, I was explaining to Jodie what she could expect from the writers coaching she would be receiving, when she suddenly said, "I have something for you!" I looked over and she was holding a beautiful, glittery, pink and white ink pen.

At first, I was hesitant, not wanting her to give up one of her possessions, until she said the next words, "I want you to have this, and I want you to know I love you. I can see that you like the things I like."

I graciously (and humbly) accepted the ink pen.

Jodie and I worked long and hard in getting her story put together. It isn't easy to continually relay something so heartbreaking, and I knew that Jodie was reliving it each time we talked. But she persevered and every time we spoke, she would tell me something else about Libbi, her husband, Willie, and their experience. She would also reveal more of her feelings in all she went through during the time Libbi was on this Earth.

Jodie and Willie are thankful for the short time they were able to spend with Libbi. She has assured me they will try to have more children in the future. She repeats her motto: *Healthy Mom, Healthy Baby*, and fully believes it.

Jodie knows they won't replace Libbi, but she thanks God for the time they were able to have with her, and they thank Him for the next baby He will allow them to have. She looks forward to that day.

~ Shelley Wilburn

Bonus Material

Angel Heart

Angel Heart 5-Day Devotional

Day 1: Waiting is the Hardest Part

Trust in the LORD with all your heart, And lean not on your own understanding; In all your ways acknowledge Him, And He shall direct your paths.
~ Proverbs 3:5-6, NKJV

Are you good at waiting? I believe everyone can say, "At times I am, but too often I'm not."

In Proverbs 3:5-6, we are instructed to do three things:
1. Trust in the LORD.
2. Don't trust in ourselves.
3. Acknowledge Him in everything.

If we do those three things, it says God will direct our paths.

When we find ourselves in a precarious situation; illness, financial struggle, loss, grief, etc., it can be easy to make quick decisions without taking time to pray or trust in the LORD.

The first part of Proverbs 3:5 tells us about trusting the LORD – to trust Him with all our heart. That means with everything inside and outside of us.

If we trust Him with everything – with our whole

heart – we will begin to notice, we react to our circumstances much differently.

For example, instead of anxiety, stress, or impatience, we begin to experience peace.

"Don't worry about anything; instead, pray about everything. Tell God what you need, and thank Him for all he has done," Philippians 4:6, NLT.

In the above verse, we are told to be anxious for nothing. It sounds hard, but if we take everything to God in prayer and petition, then thank Him, he makes a promise to us in the next verse.

"Then you will experience God's peace, which exceeds anything we can understand. His peace will guard your hearts and minds as you live in Christ Jesus," Philippians 4:7, NLT.

Peace in times of chaos confuses many, including the enemy (the devil). But that is our opportunity to show Jesus to those around us.

When we are presented with circumstances that threaten our life, home, family or anything else, it can be easy to begin to focus on the negative, or the stress of the moment.

Hear me when I say, it's okay to be upset, to cry, to be angry or even afraid. These are all natural parts of life. My point is that, even though we may feel these things, it's important that we don't allow them to control us or our actions. Instead, take those things to God and allow Him to help us through our situation.

Whenever those overwhelming feelings try to overtake us, the important thing to do is found in

Philippians 4:8 from the New Living Translation:

"And now, dear brothers and sisters, one final thing. Fix your thoughts on what is true, and honorable, and right, and pure, and lovely, and admirable. Think about things that are excellent and worthy of praise."

It may seem difficult to focus on those, but we do have a Helper who will be with us and guide us. His name is *Jesus*.

When we think about, or put all our focus on Jesus, the troubles of this life dim in comparison. Also, when we acknowledge Him in all our ways, then He begins to direct our paths (Proverbs 3:5), making the "crooked places straight" (Isaiah 45:2a), and leading us "beside still waters" (Psalms 23:2b).

At times, waiting may be hard. Yet, when we focus on Jesus, we find He gives us peace as He leads us through the valley (Psalms 23:4).

Day 2: Guard Your Heart

Guard your heart above all else, for it determines the course of your life. ~ Proverbs 4:23, NLT

Guarding your heart is often misconstrued or misunderstood. Many times, we think that, to guard our heart is to separate ourselves from others so we don't get hurt.

In truth, it's when we pull away and separate ourselves that we make ourselves open and vulnerable to be hurt.

Let me explain it like this: The devil wants us separated. He wants us alone, so he can whisper lies to us, trying to convince us that we are alone, no one wants us or loves us, and the greatest lie he whispers is that God has turned His back on us.

Lies, lies, lies!

The Bible teaches us that we are never alone.

"Do not be afraid or discouraged, for the LORD will personally go ahead of you. He will be with you; he will neither fail you nor abandon you," ~ Deuteronomy 31:8, NLT.

Sometimes, we may feel rejected and alone, especially during difficult times. Many of those times, we do need some alone time in order to process our thoughts, to pray, or to get into God's Word and allow Him to speak into our heart and soul.

When we do come into those times, we need to remember to guard our heart, to pay attention to the things we begin to think, or to those whispers inside.

Be sure we discern whether it is from our Heavenly Father or the enemy. How? Read the Word.

"The Lord will not reject his people; he will not

abandon his special possession," ~ Psalms 94:14, NLT.

Knowing God will not reject or abandon us is comforting. But what makes my heart soar is learning I am his special possession. So are you, my friend!

The next time you begin to think upsetting thoughts, or feel as if you're alone, remember, those are lies from the evil one, the devil – and remember what Jesus said about the devil: *"...he is a liar and the father of lies," John 8:44, NLT.*

The best way to guard your heart and kick the devil out comes from James chapter four. We are given a few steps to take. Read below.

"So humble yourselves before God. Resist the devil, and he will flee from you. Come close to God, and God will come close to you," ~ James 4:7-8a, NLT.

When we humble ourselves first, before God, He notices. So does the devil. But when we resist the devil, he will flee – run away – from us.

Don't celebrate just yet. Once he leaves, verse eight says to come close to God and He will come close to us. However, there is one more thing we are told to do, in the last part of verse eight.

"Wash your hands, you sinners; purify your hearts, for your loyalty is divided between God and the world." ~ James 4:8b, NLT.

Don't let your loyalty be divided between God and the world. Divided loyalty is when we say we follow God, or worship God, then go out during the week and live by worldly standards. That can be in the shows we watch on TV, things we view on the internet, the way we talk, or the way we speak to or treat others, etc.

If you find yourself saying or doing things that don't line up with God's Word, *repent*. Ask God to forgive you, and He will!

"But if we confess our sins to him, he is faithful and just to forgive us our sins and to cleanse us from all wickedness," ~ 1 John 1:9, NLT.

Then make a conscious effort to not do those things anymore. That's what it means to wash your hands and purify your heart.

Guard your heart by staying close to God. Also, the best way to resist the enemy is to declare God's Word over your life and the lives of those you love. Do it *out loud*, because the enemy cannot hear your thoughts. He only whispers lies into your mind, trying to get you to doubt God. But, when you humble yourself before God, when you come close to Him, in turn, He will do something for you.

"Humble yourselves before the Lord, and he will lift you up in honor." ~ James 4:10, NLT

Day 3: The Strength of My Heart

My flesh and my heart fail; But God is the strength of my heart and my portion forever. ~ Psalms 73:26, NKJV

Life often has a way of dragging us down. We must remember though, we are only traveling through this life, in this world. This is not our permanent stopping point.

As Psalms 73:26 above says, "My flesh and my heart fail…". As a spirit in human flesh (which that's what we are) this flesh is going to fail. We are going to have moments when we are going to make mistakes.

When it says our hearts fail, it doesn't always mean physical heart; although sometimes, in some people, like Libbi, their physical heart does fail. However, more often than not, this means our spiritual heart fails. That's when we are making mistakes, having wrong mindsets, thoughts, words, actions, how we treat others, etc.

What I find encouraging is the next sentence, especially how it begins: *But God…* We fail every day. But God.

It goes on to say that He is the strength of our heart. He is the One who gives us strength, encouragement; He picks us up, dusts us off, and points us back on the right path going in the right direction.

More than that, He helps us feel better in our heart (our feelings) and in our mind and body.

Even more than that, if it couldn't get any better – it can, because even though God helps us, He also lets us know that He is the strength of our heart. It's not our own strength (although some do believe they do things on their own – they don't). Our strength comes from God. It's His.

Therefore, He is our strength, and He is our portion: He is ours; faithful, firm, trustworthy, forever. I find this extremely encouraging.

Let's look at the word *forever*. So many times, we think God has abandoned us. Again, this is a lie from the enemy!

When God says "forever," He means it. Forever is eternal, never-ending. So, if God is our portion forever, we can't get rid of Him! He is always there. Nothing can cause Him to step away from us or stop loving us.

Romans 8:38-39 (NLT) says, *"And I am convinced that nothing can ever separate us from God's love. Neither death nor life, neither angels nor demons, neither our fears for today nor our worries about tomorrow – not even the powers of hell can separate us from God's love. No power in the sky above or in the earth below – indeed, nothing in all creation will ever be able to separate us from the love of God that is revealed in Christ Jesus our Lord."*

Of course, we often step away or turn away from God, but He never stops loving us!

However, when we repent and turn back to Him, we find Him waiting with open arms.

To some, they may find that hard to believe. Let me give you some hope today. God does love you, and He cannot lie, therefore, He can be trusted.

"So God has given both his promise and his oath. These two things are unchangeable because it is impossible for God to lie. Therefore, we who have fled to him for refuge can have great confidence as we hold to the hope that lies before us," ~ Hebrews 6:19, NTL.

"This truth gives them confidence that they have eternal life, which God – who does not lie – promised them before the world began," ~ Titus 1:2, NLT.

Let these verses strengthen (encourage) your heart today.

Day 4: The LORD is Close

The LORD is close to the brokenhearted; he rescues those whose spirits are crushed. ~ Psalms 34:18, NLT

Isn't it heartwarming to know that, whenever our hearts are broken, the LORD is close to us?

It makes me think of times when my kids were small, and something would happen to upset them. Their little hearts were broken. They would climb in my lap for hugs and snuggles. Though the tears fell, they knew Mommy was close. Before long, they felt better and, after one more squeeze, wipe of the tears, and blow of the nose, they were ready to go back to play.

As adults, we don't find ourselves getting to have those moments to have the hugs and snuggles… not physically, at least. But when we are upset, or our hearts are broken, Jesus is even closer to us.

In Psalms 34:18, above, it even says He rescues us when our spirits are crushed.

In verse seventeen, it says He hears us when we call to him for help, and He rescues us from *all* our troubles. The interesting thing about that word *all* is that, in any language, especially the Greek and Hebrew, all means… *ALL*. Not one thing is left out.

In verse nineteen, it says we face many troubles. Yet it goes on to encourage by saying, *"… but the LORD comes to the rescue each time."*

Each time! That means *all* the time. *Every* time.

How uplifting! To know that every time we are discouraged, heartbroken, hurt, in trials or trouble, whatever it is that has us vexed, *when* we call out to

Jesus, *He is there*. He rescues us every time, without fail.

Day 5: Healing the Brokenhearted

He heals the brokenhearted And binds up their wounds. ~ Psalms 147:3, NKJV

Since we are still encouraged from the last devotion, let's continue in it, knowing that the Lord also heals us when we are brokenhearted, and binds up our wounds (Psalms 147:3).

This speaks volumes to me. If you know my story, you know of my healing from severe depression and anxiety. But something I don't talk much about is the emotional trauma behind it.

Growing up, there were many times I found myself broken over words and actions which were directed at me. In those hopeless moments, although I felt heartbroken, there was something else happening: my wounds were being bound by an unseen force which I couldn't explain. I later learned it was the Lord binding my wounds.

How could that happen? I had a praying grandmother.

We can do the same for others who are brokenhearted and bruised. We, too, can be the hands and feet of Jesus in that we pray for those whose hearts are broken. While Jesus binds up their wounds, we can supply the love and support they need as they heal.

We can remind them that, by the stripes of Jesus, they are healed (2 Peter 2:24). We can help them know that the weapons the enemy is forming against them will not succeed, and they can silence the words being spoken in accusation, to and about them. We can remind them that their vindication comes from the

Lord. This is not only a promise, but these are benefits we can enjoy because we are servants of the Lord (Isaiah 54:17).

Whenever any of us goes through heartbreaking events, we have the opportunity to show love to one another.

"Love means doing what God has commanded us, and he has commanded us to love one another, just as you heard from the beginning," ~ 2 John 1:6, NLT.

We are to also pray for each other.

"Confess your sins to each other and pray for each other so that you may be healed. The earnest prayer of a righteous person has great power and produces wonderful results," ~ James 5:16, NLT.

This is not only our benefit, but our right, our privilege, as well as our assignment from Jesus. What a wonderful opportunity we have to help Him build the Kingdom of God by showing love and praying for those around us.

May you be blessed as you lift each other in love and prayer.

APPENDIX A

Understanding Grief
from Tina Porter, M.A., QMHP, B.S.W.,
Grief, Trauma & Mental Health Expert

What is Grief? Grief vs. Grieving

Grief
- Grief is the natural response to loss.
- Grief is the emotional and psychological reaction to the loss of someone or something that a person loved and/or cared deeply about.
- Grief is the emotional suffering you may feel when something or someone you love is taken away from you.
- Grief is the wave that comes and knocks you off your feet or knocks you and your life off balance, and it strikes the very core of you.
- Grief is deep sorrow, sadness and anguish.

Grieving
- Grieving is the experience of "grief feelings" that change over time but doesn't go away.
- Grieving becomes a big part of your life, and as to how you will now function and live with the loss.
- Grieving is a process, and it is something that you will have to live with and gradually move through the various stages of grief throughout a lifetime.
- Grieving is a lifelong process because it is simply the expression of your unending love for the person who has died.

The 5 Stages of Grief and the Grieving Process (Elisabeth Kubler-Ross Grief Cycle)

- Denial – disbelief, avoidance, confusion, elation, shock, fear.
- Anger – frustration, irritation, anxiety.

- Bargaining – struggling to find meaning, negotiating with God, hope that the situation could change for an exchange.

- Depression – overwhelmed, hopeless, helplessness, hostility, withdrawn, flight, feelings of being detached from others and the world.

- Acceptance – exploring options, new plan, have gained a sense of peace and meaning, developed a new perception, have a new plan in place, moving on or forward in life with accepting what has happened and accepting the loss.

Everyone Grieves Differently

- Grief is personal. Grieve the way you need to in your own way. This is your grief journey and no one else's.
- There is no right or wrong way to grieve.
- There is no timeframe on grief. Grieve at your own pace. Everyone responds or reacts to grief differently.
- Grief is very complex.
- Grief is the most difficult thing in life that humans have to face.
- You do not have to grieve the way others want or expect you to grieve.
- Grief is a slow, gradual transformative process.
- Research studies have shown that on the average, typically, most people are adjusting to grief at about twelve (12) months and feel more stabilized. However, the grieving journey is a lifetime.

Some Feelings of Grief

- Feeling overwhelmed
- Numb
- Shocked
- Anger
- Disbelief
- Guilt
- Profound sadness
- Empty inside
- Unstable
- Anxious
- Scared
- Irritable
- Hopeless
- Yearning
- Helpless
- Lonely
- Depressed
- Frustrated
- Detached

Spiritual Effects of Grief

- Feel let down by God, blame God for allowing the loss to occur, angry with God.
- May feel like God is angry with you, or He is punishing you.
- Confused about Faith.
- Doubt about God.
- Disruption in Spiritual, Faith or Religious Practices.
- Question your faith that you've always had prior to the loss.
- Perhaps, if one did not have a particular faith or religious belief system before, pull even further away from the belief

of the existence of God or just Spirituality in general.
• Some feel more drawn to God and want to connect to God for comfort and hope and yearn for Heaven or divine encounters or experiences.
• Some may even feel the need to become more spiritual, have the need to pray and meditate more, research the spiritual realm, learn more about God, want to be more present spiritually and connect with inner spirit more or connect with a spiritual or faith community.
• May feel the need to pray, meditate, read holy, biblical Scriptures, research about an afterlife to find peace and meaning, as a way to gain hope and their loved one is alive in Heaven with God.
• Some rely on God for strength and as a Guide and help through stress.

Myths About Grief and False Statements

• After specific period of time, you should or will be over it. Time heals all things, or time heals all wounds.
• What did not hurt last year will not hurt you this year.
• Avoid the pain and it won't hurt you.
• Crying only makes it worse.
• Talking about the loss only makes it worse.
• Grief and mourning are the same thing.
• Grief happens in orderly stages.
• Grief is the same, regardless of the loss you experience.
• It takes a year to get over grief.
• When grief is resolved, it never comes up again.

Facts About Grief

• Grief is universal.
• Death and Grief are imminent. Just as you cannot avoid death, you also cannot avoid grief.

- You cannot change what has already happened.
- Whatever you're feeling at any given moment is what you are supposed to be feeling at that moment.
- Your relationships with others will change.
- You can survive grief.
- Grief is normal.
- Grief is *yours*.
- The way out of grief is through it, going through the grief process.
- Grief is to be experienced and the pain of loss needs to be experienced.
- Allowing yourself and giving yourself permission to feel during grief is okay.
- Your grief is intimately connected to the relationship in which you had with the person whom you lost.
- Grief is hard work but is necessary.
- Processing grief by talking about it and expressing feelings to others is healthy.
- Grief comes in waves at spontaneous times throughout a lifetime.
- You learn to adapt to grief and function in life with Grief.
- Everybody does not grieve at the same time nor grieves in the same way.
- Everyone grieves differently and responds to grief differently.

How to Comfort Someone Who is Grieving

- Give the person who is grieving space and time to talk.
- Be a good listener – Actively listen.
- Respect the person's way of grieving.
- Accept mood swings.
- Avoid giving advice, rather, empathize with their grief.
- Refrain from trying to explain the loss.
- Be a help to them with practical tasks.
- Be available, present, and connected. Your presence

speaks louder than anything else and is needed, because a grieving person needs to know that they are not alone.

Moving on with Life: You Determine Readiness to Move On

• Realization that the person lost is not coming back.
• Develop new ways of relating to the deceased person.
• Learn to exist without the person.
• Acknowledging and understanding the loss.
• Keeping the loved one alive as a memory in a healthy and appropriate manner.
• Form a new identity without the person's physical presence in your life.
• Develop a new relationship with the person lost by remembering their impact and achievements in life and carry on their legacy.

APPENDIX B

Libbi's Song

We'll never forget the moment we learned of your heart.
That overwhelming feeling swept over us like a rollercoaster.
We cried and cried and said, "Why God? What did we do?"
But we…

Chorus:
Put it in God's hands.
He has a big plan for us.
So, we put it in God's hands,
Because we know He is our trust.

We'll never forget the moment when you arrived.
That painful feeling swept over us with excruciating joy.
We cried and cried and said, "You're so perfect. There's no one like you."
And we…

Chorus:
Put it in God's hands.
He has a big plan for us.
So, we put it in God's hands,
Because we know He is our trust.

We'll never forget these moments here with you.
That peaceful feeling sweeps over us like a gentle

wave.
We smile and smile and say, "You're veery special, loved, and blessed."
And we...

Chorus:
Put it in God's hands.
He has a big plan for us.
So, we put it in God's hands,
Because we know He is our trust.

Put it in God's hands.
He has a big plan for us.
So, we put it in God's hands,
Because we know He is our trust.

Put it in God's hands.
He has a big plan for us.
He has a big plan for us.

APPENDIX C

The Speeches

Mommy's Speech

Everyone knows I don't like to get up and do a speech. I get nervous doing one in a big crowd staring at me. But before I did my big speech before the crowd, I prayed and asked God to help me. He knows I'm nervous and in shock. Pray! Practice!

I did it and wasn't nervous. I acted like no one was watching me. First thing before the speech, we listened to Libbi's Song, that her mommy, daddy, and music therapy wrote about her heart.

"Never forget the moment we learned about her heart, we put it in God's hands, and we cry, cry, cry."

I know God was there for me and Willie. We are forever till we get to Heaven with our sweet baby girl, Libbi Grace Stevenson!

Final Speech

I'm not really the one to do a speech but I would first like to say, thank you, to all of you for coming to support our Libbi Grace.

Today, I am going to talk about my/our beautiful daughter. When me and your dad found out about your heart, we cried and said, "What could we have done to prevent this?" All the doctors and nurses told us that it wasn't our fault. There was not anything we could have done differently.

Libbi Grace had an amazing, unique heart. She fought every day to stay with us here on earth. She was special. She was encouraging. She taught people how to pray!

Mommy and Daddy's plans were to bring you home, Libbi. Your first birthday party was going to be Strawberry Shortcake, because you were "berry" sweet. We would spend Daddy's money and go shopping to boutiques and Dillard's. But God had different plans for you. He had a better plan. Of course, she would be in church with her cute outfit.

Libbi has a brand-new heart in Heaven. So, family and friends, today is a day of salvation! Forever and ever, we can know we can be in Heaven with our sweet, beautiful girl. No more disgusting machines or wires or tubes. Mommy and Daddy can't wait to see you again in that big, wonderful mansion in Gloryland.

Well done, baby girl. We love you forever and you will always be in Mommy and Daddy's hearts.

ENDNOTES

Introduction

1 Waiting is the Hardest Part
Proverbs 3:5, New King James Version
The Joy and the Hurt
Complications

2 Born Too Early
Proverbs 4:23, New Living Translation
Guard Your Heart

3 Tiny Fighter
Psalms 73:26, New King James Version
June 14, 2022

4 Saying Goodbye
Psalms 34:18, New Living Translation

5 Final Farewell
Psalms 147:3, New King James Version

Message From Jodie

Afterword

Bonus Material – Angel Heart 5-Day Devotional
Day 1 – Waiting is the Hardest Part
Proverbs 3:5-6, New King James Version
Philippians 4:7, New Living Translation
Philippians 4:8, New Living Translation
Proverbs 3:5, New King James Version
Isaiah 45:2a, New King James Version

Psalms 23:2b, New King James Version
Psalms 23:4, New King James Version

Day 2 – Guard Your Heart
Proverbs 4:23, New Living Translation
Deuteronomy 31:8, New Living Translation
Psalms 94:14, New Living Translation
John 8:44, New Living Translation
James 4:7-8a, New Living Translation
James 4:8b, New Living Translation
1 John 1:9, New Living Translation
James 4:10, New Living Translation

Day 3 – The Strength of My Heart
Psalms 73:26, New King James Version
Romans 8:38-39, New Living Translation
Hebrews 6:19, New Living Translation
Titus 1:2, New Living Translation

Day 4 – The LORD is Close
Psalms 34:18, New Living Translation
Psalms 34:19, New Living Translation

Day 5 – Healing the Brokenhearted
Psalms 147:3, New King James Version
2 Peter 2:24, New Living Translation
Isaiah 54:17, New Living Translation
2 John 1:6, New Living Translation
James 5:16, New Living Translation

Appendix A
Understanding Grief, from Pain to Purpose, by Tina Porter, M.A., QMHP, B.S.W, Trauma and Mental Health Expert

5-Stages of Grief and the Grieving Process, Elisabeth Kubler-Ross Grief Cycle

**Appendix B
The Speeches**

Endnotes

About the Author

Other Titles by Shelley Wilburn

Picture Gallery

About the Author

Shelley Wilburn is no novice when it comes to writing. She has been writing since she was twelve years old. She has authored several books, including the Walking Healed series, written for newspapers and women's magazines, written several articles and newsletters, as well as co-authored devotionals. She has also become a Ghost (ghostwriting for others), and her most recent endeavor, launching her editing and publishing business, Mountain Joy Publishing, where she coaches new writers and helps them launch their writing career. In addition to writing, Shelley is also an avid reader, book reviewer, blogger, and speaker. She is the founder and president of Walking Healed Ministries, which helps people who struggle with depression and anxiety to find healing and wholeness through Jesus Christ. Shelley lives in Southern Illinois with her husband of more than forty years, Don, and their two hilarious Chihuahuas, Georgie and Tootsie, and their Great Pyrenees, Grizzy.

Shelley loves to hear from her readers.

You can find Shelley at:
Her website: www.shelleywilburn.org
Facebook: www.facebook.com/authorshelleywilburn
Instagram: www.instagram.com/shelleywilburn
Email her at: mountainjoypublishing@gmail.com

Other Titles by Shelley Wilburn

Walking Healed, A Journey of Forgiveness, Grace, and Hope

Written in diary form, Shelley Wilburn's book, Walking Healed is her journey after being healed from over Forty years of mental and emotional abuse, as well as severe depression, anxiety and intimidation. Using snippets of her healing journey along with biblical truths, Shelley takes the reader on a journey of healing, forgiveness, grace, hope, and then leads into finding your purpose.

Written for those who suffer the pain and loneliness of depression and intimidation, Shelley reaches down into the black hold, finds those who are hurting, and helps them find their way out.

Walking Healed will help the reader realize that even Christians suffer depression. Shelley Wilburn knows and understands this from her personal experience. She also knows the freedom from these issues when God heals you and takes you on a wonderful journey of walking healed. Shelley's story of healing helps others know that even depression is curable and "nothing is impossible with God."

Walking Healed Companion Study

As a companion to Walking Healed, the Walking Healed Companion Bible Study is a five-week journey into discovering healing, forgiveness, grace, hope, and finding your purpose. Designed to be used in conjunction with the Walking Healed book, Shelley Wilburn leads you into the depths of the Bible to discover healing for whatever holds you captive. She will then lead you in discovering forgiveness, God's grace, and the hope He gives us. In the final week, you will begin to discover your purpose in life.

Walking healed and its companion study is designed to help women (and men) break free and live the life God intended for them.

Warrior Princess: Ignite Your Inner Warrior

One of the foundational principles in life is to understand who we are and what our purpose is in this life. But often, we find ourselves floundering.

Warrior Princess is a powerful, call-to-action Bible study for women, with journal and coloring pages tucked within the eight-week plan, that takes you on an interactive journey to discover your identity according to God's Word. Designed to awaken the inner warrior within the depths of your soul Warrior Princess will help you discover that you were chosen, and planned for, even before the foundations of the world, and what it truly means to be a daughter of the Most High God.

The Healing Path, A 30-Day Guide to Walking Healed and Living in Freedom

The Healing Path, a thirty-day devotional, is full of encouraging stories. Shelley Wilburn enlists the help of a few close friends as they take you on a deep dive into God's Word to illuminate the path before you. Inside, you will discover how to find healing and freedom from the obstacles that keep you from living in an abundant and enjoyable life. At the end of each day's devotion, you will also find further readings, Lights for Your Path, to illuminate your way to help keep you on the right path continuing your journey of walking healed and living in freedom.

O Mighty Warrior! Igniting the Warrior Within

Taken from Warrior Princess, O Mighty Warrior! was written for men who don't seem to realize they have spiritual authority to do the things God has called them to do. A powerful call-to-action journey, O Mighty Warrior! is a call for men to stand in their spiritual authority as men, spiritual leaders of their home, as well as igniting the warrior within them. O Mighty Warrior! will help men to discover that they were chosen even before the foundations of the world.

Angel Heart

Picture Gallery

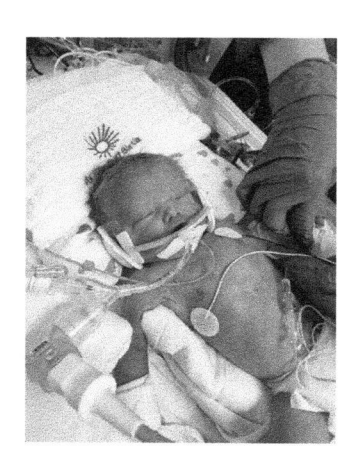

Angel Heart

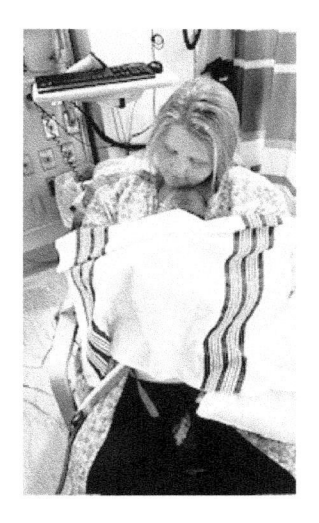

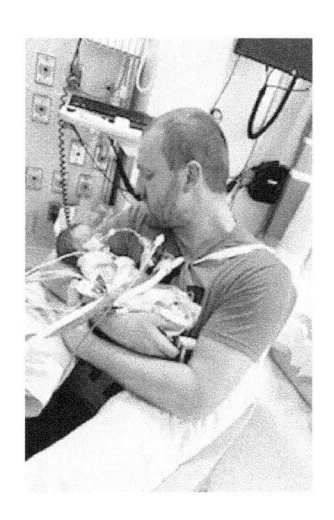

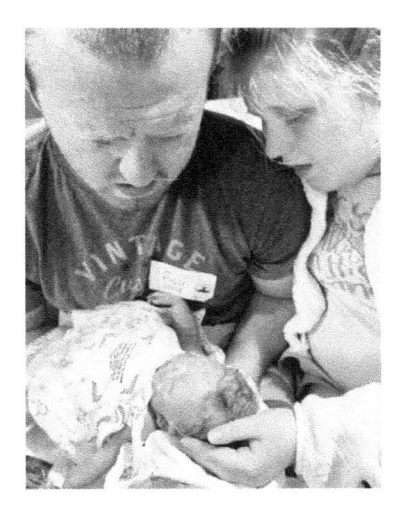

Opposite Page: Left; Jodie and Willie, Prom. Right, Wedding Day.
Bottom left; Gender Reveal (It's a Girl!). Bottom right; Libbi.

Upper Left: In the NICU, Jodie holding Libbi. Upper Right, Willie holding Libbi. Bottom: Willie and Jodie holding Libbi for the last time.